Looking at Literature Through Primary Sources™

Johnny Tremain and the American Revolution

Corona Brezina

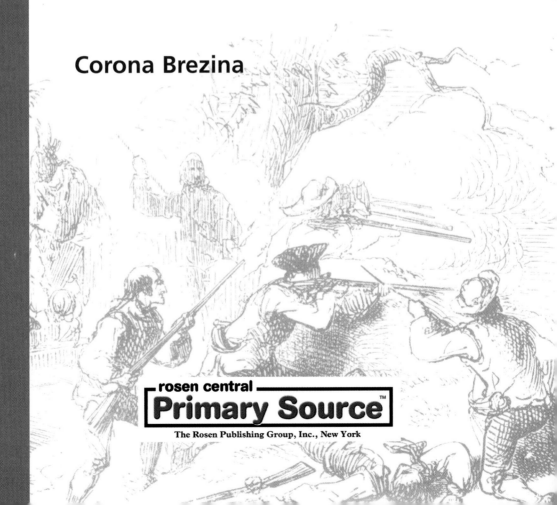

rosen central
Primary Source™
The Rosen Publishing Group, Inc., New York

Published in 2004 by The Rosen Publishing Group, Inc.
29 East 21st Street, New York, NY 10010

First Edition

Unless otherwise attributed, all quotes in this book are excerpted from *Johnny Tremain: A Novel for Old and Young*.

Library of Congress Cataloging-in-Publication Data

Brezina, Corona.
Johnny Tremain and the American Revolution/Corona Brezina.—1st ed.
    p. cm.—(Looking at literature through primary sources)
Summary: Traces the process and influences behind the writing of Esther Forbes's novel, *Johnny Tremain*, for which she won a Newbery Award in 1943—just a year after winning the Pulitzer Prize for her first novel.
Includes bibliographical references.
ISBN 0-8239-4504-9
1. Forbes, Esther. *Johnny Tremain*. 2. United States—History—Revolution, 1775–1783—Literature and the revolution. 3. Historical fiction, American—History and criticism. 4. Children's stories, American—History and criticism. 5. Literature and history—United States. 6. Boston (Mass.)—In literature. [1. Forbes, Esther. *Johnny Tremain*—Sources. 2. United States—History—Revolution, 1775–1783–Literature and the revolution. 3. American literature—History and criticism.]
I. Title. II. Series.
PS3511.O3495J6533 2004
813'.52—dc22

                                               2003014989

Manufactured in the United States of America

On the cover: at top, a 1937 photograph of Esther Forbes; at bottom left, a 1789 engraving by W. D. Cooper depicting the Boston Tea Party; at bottom right, the cover of the first edition of *Johnny Tremain*.

CONTENTS

INTRODUCTION

In 1943, Esther Forbes published her classic *Johnny Tremain: A Novel for Old and Young*. It became an instant hit and won the prestigious Newbery Medal for children's books. Readers already knew Forbes's name. The previous year, she had won the Pulitzer Prize for her nonfiction work *Paul Revere and the World He Lived In*. It was unheard of that a little-known author would win both prizes, one following the other!

Esther Forbes was born on June 28, 1891, in Westborough, Massachusetts. When she was seven years old, her family moved to the historic town of Worcester, Massachusetts, which is close to Boston. The citizens of Worcester had defied the British before the Revolutionary War and stockpiled military supplies. Forbes left Worcester to attend the University of Wisconsin, and she returned to Worcester to work for the Houghton Mifflin publishing company. She wrote her first book in 1926 and others followed. Forbes moved away from Worcester during her seven-year marriage to Albert Hoskins. After their divorce, she returned to Worcester, this time permanently, in 1933.

Esther Forbes, pictured here with her dog Sir Tristam in February 1937, won the 1943 Pulitzer Prize in History for her book *Paul Revere and the World He Lived In*. *Johnny Tremain* was awarded the Newbery Medal in 1944. Named for eighteenth-century British bookseller John Newbery, this award is given each year for the most distinguished contribution to American literature for children.

Her mother, Harriette Merrifield Forbes, was also a writer and historian. Esther Forbes had dyslexia and poor eyesight. When she started writing about Paul Revere, Harriette helped her daughter by studying letters, newspapers, and other eighteenth-century documents. Forbes did not have to travel far to find documents from the Revolution. Massachusetts was a center of rebellion leading up to the war, and records had been well preserved by historians and historical societies in the state.

Artist Lynd Ward created this portrait of Johnny Tremain for the first edition of the book. Highly acclaimed, Ward illustrated many award-winning books. He won the Caldecott Medal in 1953 and the Regina Award in 1975. Ward worked until he died in 1985.

Johnny Tremain was published during World War II, a patriotic time for Americans. This is reflected in Forbes's portrayal of the patriots in the prerevolutionary colonies. Some historians have questioned the patriots' motives in working for American independence. Forbes depicts Sam Adams and other leaders as honorable men working for a worthy cause. For boys growing up during the American Revolution, they offered a vision of an independent America worth fighting for.

Chapter 1

Boyhood in the American Colonies

The first chapter of *Johnny Tremain* opens in the summer of 1773. The British governed the American colonies, and Bostonians had few complaints about their rule. The city had been far more tense three years before. After the French and Indian War ended in 1763, the British had tried to make American colonists pay to support British troops stationed in the colonies. They added taxes to many imports. The colonists, especially Bostonians, resisted the taxes and boycotted British goods. At the height of the colonists' outrage, in 1770, British soldiers fired on a mob of protesters and killed five Americans. This event became known as the Boston Massacre. The British repealed many of the tax measures, and the citizens of Boston quieted down. Many people, like Johnny, took little interest in politics.

Near the beginning of the book, Johnny Tremain, a young silversmith apprentice, burns and cripples his hand on molten silver. Johnny lives with the Lapham family, which includes a grandfather, his daughter-in-law, four granddaughters, and three apprentices. The reader learns about the daily routine in eighteenth-century America. After Johnny burns his hand and

On March 5, 1770, five men were shot and killed in Boston by British soldiers, in an event known as the Boston Massacre. This engraving by Paul Revere is based on drawings by Henry Pelham. Copies of Revere's engraving were already for sale by the time Pelham's prints hit the street. Both promote the patriots' cause, although they are short on accuracy. For example, Crispus Attucks was a black man killed in the attack. In this print, he is shown as a white man lying on the ground closest to the British soldiers.

can no longer work, he wanders around aimlessly, and Forbes describes eighteenth-century Boston.

Esther Forbes introduces many of her main characters in the early chapters, focusing especially on the bright but haughty Johnny. Before his accident, Johnny had been Lapham's most talented apprentice.

> It was over a year since he had carried charcoal or a bucket of water, touched a broom or helped Mrs. Lapham brew ale. His ability made him semi-sacred. He knew his power and reveled in it. He could have easily made friends with stupid Dove, for Dove was lonely and admired Johnny as well as envied him. Johnny preferred to bully him.

Besides her fictional characters, Forbes also introduces two important real-life patriots. The wealthy John Hancock was a key revolutionary leader who eventually spent much of his fortune supplying the minutemen with arms and ammunition. He became the first signer of the Declaration of Independence in 1776. Paul Revere, best known for his midnight ride, mastered trades from silversmithing and engraving to making false teeth during his lifetime. His copperplate engravings, including one of the Boston Massacre, drew public attention to the patriots' cause.

Forbes's cast includes people from all social classes, including artisans, servants, and rich gentlemen. Johnny's life changes after he pays a visit to the fictional Tory merchant Jonathan

And it is not unlikely to be an armed Cutter bound hither, one or two of them being daily expected.

WHEREAS many Perſons are ſo unfortunate as to loſe their Fore-Teeth by Accident, and otherways, to their great Detriment, not only in Looks, but ſpeaking both in Public and Private :—This is to inform all ſuch, that they may have them re-placed with artificial Ones, that looks as well as the Natural, & anſwers the End of Speaking to all Intents, by PAUL REVERE, Goldſmith, near the Head of Dr. Clarke's Wharf, Boſton.
₊ All Perſons who have had falſe Teeth fixt by Mr. John Baker, Surgeon-Dentiſt, and they have got looſe (as they will in Time) may have them faſtened by the above, who learnt the Method of fixing them from Mr. Baker.

Boſton, Printed by EDES & GILL,

A fine silversmith, Revere also worked as a dentist, as seen in this ad *(left)*, which ran in the *Boston Gazette* on September 19, 1768. The portrait of Paul Revere *(right)* was painted between 1768 and 1770 by one of America's finest painters, John Singleton Copley. Revere was an outspoken patriot. Copley was a Loyalist and thought the colonies should remain loyal to the British king.

Lyte and shows him a silver cup left to him by his mother. The Tories, also called Loyalists, supported British rule in the colonies. Instead of recognizing him as a relation, Lyte accuses Johnny of stealing the cup and has him arrested. Johnny's brilliant lawyer, Josiah Quincy, is remembered today for defending the British soldiers charged after the Boston Massacre when no one else would represent them. Nonetheless, he was an ardent Whig, supportive of independence for the colonies. Johnny recognized that "his cough was prophetic of an early death." Quincy died of tuberculosis two years later.

After being acquitted, Johnny foolishly returns to Lyte and tries to sell him the cup, his last valuable possession. Lyte takes the cup without paying for it. In a rage, Johnny runs to the *Boston Observer* print shop and asks for a job as a message boy. Johnny first meets Sam Adams, who Forbes calls "the most powerful man in Boston," while delivering papers. Adams was a master of political intrigue who urged Bostonians to resist the British rather than compromise. One of the greatest political writers of his day, he almost single-handedly united Americans against the British before the Revolution.

Johnny encounters a number of important leaders in Boston during the time before the Boston Tea Party. John Adams, the future president, and Dr. Joseph Warren both attend gatherings of the fictional Boston Observers. Dr. Warren, the popular and able doctor who worked passionately

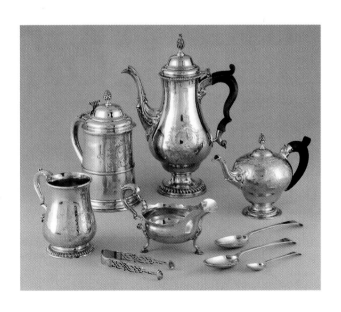

◆◆◆ **Shown here is a tea set crafted by Paul Revere in 1773. It is considered one of the finest examples of silver work produced in eighteenth-century New England. It was commissioned by Dr. William Paine for his bride, Lois Orne.**

for American freedom, would later die in the Battle of Bunker Hill. Forbes also introduces James Otis and Dr. Benjamin Church. Otis had been the first leader to champion the rights of American colonists but became mentally unstable in 1769. Johnny feels that Dr. Church is crooked, though he has no evidence. In late 1775,

This portrait of Joseph Warren *(left)* was painted by Edward Savage after a 1765 original by John Singleton Copley. Warren was a radical patriot leader who is thought to have been one of the masterminds of the Boston Tea Party. He died at the Battle of Bunker Hill in 1775. This 1772 portrait of Samuel Adams *(right)* was painted by Copley. A tireless patriot, Samuel Adams organized the Sons of Liberty in 1765 and ran the meeting of December 16, 1773, before the Boston Tea Party occurred. A signer of the Declaration of Independence, Samuel Adams served in Congress and as governor of Massachusetts.

On August 14, 1769, the Sons of Liberty dined at the Liberty Tree in Dorchester, Massachusetts. This list, in alphabetical order, names the members of this secret group. It was compiled by member William Palfrey. The document was donated to the Massachusetts Historical Society in August 1869 by Palfrey's grandson to commemorate the 100-year anniversary of the gathering.

George Washington would arrest Dr. Church as a spy working for British general Thomas Gage.

The Sons of Liberty, which served as a model for the Observers, was the most prominent of a number of patriotic societies in Boston. The Sons of Liberty organized in 1765 in response to taxes imposed by the British Stamp Act. Group members often gathered at the Green Dragon tavern, mentioned in *Johnny Tremain*. Whigs admired the group's dedication to colonists' rights and its determination in opposing unfair British measures. The

Tories, though, considered the members a bunch of rabble-rousers intent on sabotaging the rightful British authorities.

During the months after the Boston Tea Party, Johnny joins Paul Revere's spy network watching British activities. His friends and acquaintances hold a variety of political stances. Rab Silsbee and many other patriots begin training with the Lexington minutemen. Other Bostonians, including the Lapham family, side with the Tories. Most of the British, such as Lieutenant Stranger, look forward to seeing the rebels put down. However, a British soldier named Pumpkin believes in American freedom and deserts the army. As resentment against the British grows, the Lytes are harassed in Milton at their country home and flee to Boston.

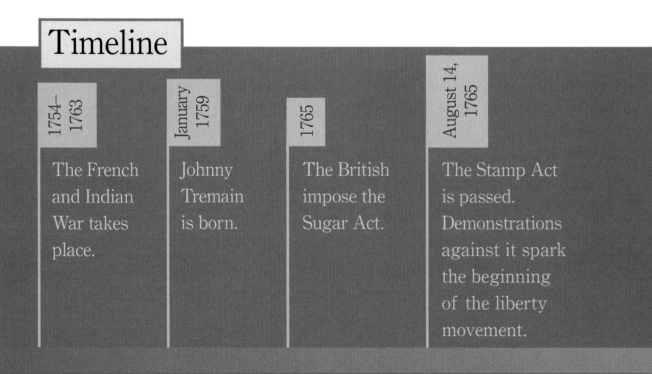

Timeline

1754–1763
The French and Indian War takes place.

January 1759
Johnny Tremain is born.

1765
The British impose the Sugar Act.

August 14, 1765
The Stamp Act is passed. Demonstrations against it spark the beginning of the liberty movement.

◆◆◆ The Green Dragon tavern was located downstairs in this building that had been purchased by the St. Andrews Lodge in 1764. Historians believe the Sons of Liberty planned the Boston Tea Party here.

The final chapters of *Johnny Tremain* describe anticipation of a British attack and the first battle of the war. Johnny helps discover the British plan to march on Lexington and Concord, and he sends Paul Revere off on his famous midnight ride. The Battle of Lexington and Concord starts the Revolution the next

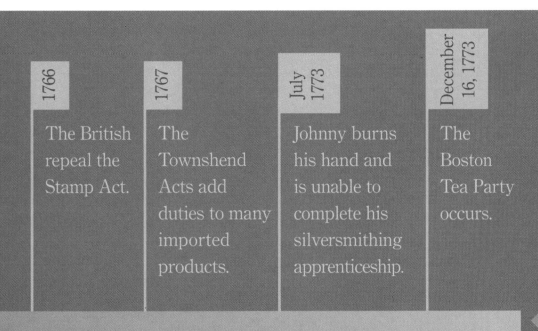

1766	1767	July 1773	December 16, 1773
The British repeal the Stamp Act.	The Townshend Acts add duties to many imported products.	Johnny burns his hand and is unable to complete his silversmithing apprenticeship.	The Boston Tea Party occurs.

morning, April 19, 1775. After the British are defeated, the Lytes leave for England and take young Isannah Lapham with them. Lavinia Lyte, merchant Jonathan Lyte's daughter, tells Johnny before she leaves that she is his distant cousin.

Johnny is no longer the arrogant child he was in the beginning of the book. His conversation with Bessie, the Lytes' Whig servant, shows how much he has changed.

> **"How old are you, Johnny?" she asked.**
> **"Sixteen."**
> **"And what's that—a boy or a man?"**
> **He laughed. "A boy in time of peace and a man in time of war."**

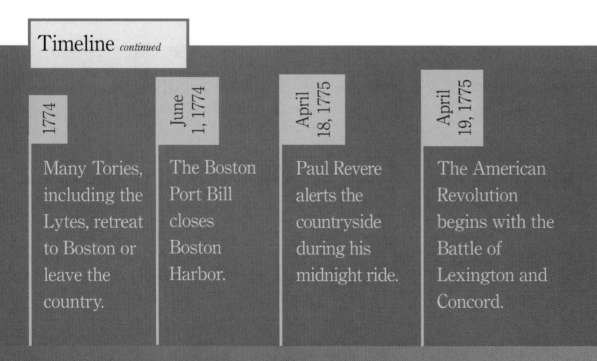

Timeline *continued*

1774
Many Tories, including the Lytes, retreat to Boston or leave the country.

June 1, 1774
The Boston Port Bill closes Boston Harbor.

April 18, 1775
Paul Revere alerts the countryside during his midnight ride.

April 19, 1775
The American Revolution begins with the Battle of Lexington and Concord.

Johnny sneaks out of Boston in search of Rab and finally finds him near the Lexington battlefield. Rab dies of his battle wounds, one of the first casualties of the war.

Johnny and the rebellious patriots face an uncertain future at the end of the book. Today, we know that the colonists stood at the brink of a hard-fought but triumphant revolution. Forbes leaves the reader to speculate on Johnny Tremain's fate.

June 17, 1775	1776	1781	1787
The Battle of Bunker Hill is fought.	The Continental Congress drafts the Declaration of Independence.	British general Charles Cornwallis surrenders at Yorktown after being defeated in the final battle of the Revolution.	The Constitutional Convention creates the Constitution.

Chapter 2

Paul Revere's Eighteenth-Century America

Esther Forbes delved into the letters and documents of the Revolutionary era for her acclaimed biography of Paul Revere. Revere wrote many letters to his wives, business associates, and other patriots. As a Son of Liberty, he undoubtedly contributed to the group's public statements of protest against British injustice. As an express rider, he delivered many key documents to and from the Boston patriots.

Paul Revere's documents hold a wealth of information, but Sam Adams, who nearly sustained the entire patriot cause through his writing, left us a greater legacy of information. He sent letters of protest to British leaders and letters of support to other Whig leaders. He wrote to the Committees of Correspondence of various cities and communities, keeping them up-to-date on his grievances against the British. Adams's personal letters reveal constant organizing and rallying of the patriots. Many other patriots also railed against the British in personal correspondence and public appeals.

Brilliant political thinkers such as James Otis first wrote about the issue of colonists' rights. Groups such as the Sons of Liberty

On January 1, 1770, the *Boston Gazette and Country Journal* listed the Loyalist merchants who "audaciously continue" to import British goods to Boston despite the boycott observed by colonial patriots as a protest against British taxes. At center top is an illustration showing a mother figure (Britannia) peacefully releasing a bird (America) from its cage.

later drew up formal resolutions against British actions. The Sons of Liberty aired their views in the *Boston Gazette*, printed by Benjamin Edes. After fleeing from Boston in 1775, Edes continued printing the paper from the nearby town of Watertown. Forbes also consulted six other Boston newspapers of the period, some with opposite viewpoints of the patriotic *Boston Gazette*.

Participants in and observers of such key events as the Boston Massacre, the Boston Tea Party, and the Battle of Lexington and Concord left written accounts. Some were formal statements, others casual descriptions to friends. Sam Adams and other patriots sent

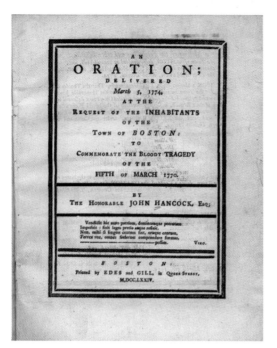

♦♦♦ John Hancock delivered the Boston Massacre Oration on March 5, 1774, to commemorate the anniversary of the bloody event. The speech reflected a changing, anti-British attitude that would lead to the American Revolution. Some historians believe that Dr. Samuel Cooper wrote the speech for Hancock. On the left is the title page of the published speech.

out messages across the colonies telling of the events and urging communities to organize against the British.

Patriots rallied crowds during speeches that could last as long as four hours. Some of these speeches were written down, though many have been lost. Even back then, busy leaders occasionally employed speechwriters. It is believed that Dr. Samuel Cooper wrote Hancock's famous speech which was made on March 5, 1774, commemorating the Boston Massacre.

The British told a very different version of the colonists' discontent. They considered America an extension of Britain and saw the patriots as troublesome British citizens. Sam Adams issued a report in 1772 called "The Rights of the Colonists." Thomas Hutchinson, the British governor of the Massachusetts Bay Colony, referred to Sam Adams in a letter as "the Grand Incendiary of the Province." He described the resolves in the document as

◆◆◆ Thomas Hutchinson, shown here around 1765, was governor of Massachusetts from 1771 to 1774. He was an outspoken Loyalist and an extremely unpopular politician. Hutchinson was forced to move to England, from where he wrote a reply to the Declaration of Independence and *The History of the Colony of Massachusetts and Province Bay.*

"tending to sedition and mutiny." The British authorities were outraged after events such as the Boston Tea Party.

Many who observed the events leading up to the war kept diaries or wrote lengthy accounts of their experiences. Benjamin Franklin and John Adams both published their autobiographies, and a number of military leaders wrote their memoirs. Mercy Otis Warren, sister of James Otis, wrote a three-volume history of the Revolution. Diaries were fashionable at the time, though the writers usually gave little thought to publication.

Everyday Life

Forbes probably had a difficult task in gathering the routine details of the colonists' daily lives. Diaries and letters offered some insight, though the writers often failed to mention day-to-day tidbits such as typical meals, how many sets of clothing they owned, or interactions with neighbors and family. Lifestyles varied between different social classes and regions. Poor colonists left even less evidence of their activities, since many were illiterate. Documents often neglect the daily lives of women, who had few rights during colonial times.

Forbes examined personal account books and records from churches and courts during her research. Marriage, birth, and death records revealed much about the Revere family and were

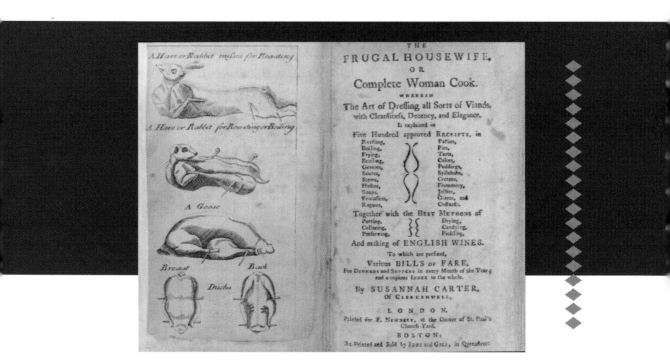

The Frugal Housewife, a popular British cookbook by Susannah Carter, was first published in London in 1772. The American version, printed the same year in Boston, contained two prints by Paul Revere. In 1796, Amelia Simmons wrote the first American cookbook. Called *American Cookery*, many of the recipes came from *The Frugal Housewife*.

typical of the average Boston family of the time. Paul Revere married Sara Orne when he was twenty-two. She was twenty-one, slightly older than the average marrying age for women. Cilla Lapham spoke accurately when she told Johnny that upon turning fifteen she was starting to think about marrying.

After sixteen years of marriage, Sara Revere died following a difficult childbirth, a common occurrence. Revere remarried a year afterward, this time to a woman ten years his junior. Many people had spouses significantly older or younger than themselves, and sometimes the woman was the older of the pair.

Altogether, Revere had sixteen children. Eleven lived to adulthood. Priscilla states that her mother considers the sickly young Isannah "not worth raising." Colonial parents loved their children, but they took it for granted that a few might die during their childhood. Many colonists lived a hard life, and doctors had a limited knowledge of many illnesses. With a handful of children and a number of pressing tasks, mothers could not always keep an eye on young children. A distressing number died in accidents.

Childhood was short in colonial America. Children dressed like adults as soon as they could walk and were given tasks as soon as they could work. Girls learned to cook, sew, and manage a household, and boys helped their fathers in their professions. Parents sometimes taught their children to read and write, though it was not considered very important for girls. Rich families sent their children to private schools of varying quality. Some rural schools taught only basic math, reading, and writing, while the best schools prepared students for life as a gentleman, scholar, or educated professional. Nine colleges had been established in the colonies by the time of the Revolution. A college education guaranteed social prestige. John Adams, Samuel Adams, and Joseph Warren all graduated from Harvard.

Boys who took apprenticeships also had to receive a basic education. Many boys served as apprentices to their fathers and eventually took over the family business. Paul Revere took his own son as an apprentice as well as boys unrelated to him. Fathers decided what trade their sons should follow, but most took the child's talents and interests into account. Traditionally, apprenticeships lasted seven years, but many boys gained the skills to find a job within four.

Boston's Slaves

Slaves made up about 10 percent of Boston's population at the time of the American Revolution. They usually lived in their owner's houses and were not as poorly treated as slaves in the Deep South. But these slaves lived very lonely lives. They rarely socialized with other slaves or free blacks, and they could seldom marry or have families of their own.

◆◆◆ Shown here is a detail of an extremely rare Paul Revere print of the college in Cambridge, New England. After making this and other prints, Revere would often reuse the copper printing plates to print money that the Massachusetts Provincial Congress needed to pay soldiers.

Working Hard from Sunup to Sundown

Forbes describes some of the typical occupations in Boston as Johnny looks for a job.

> He rarely bothered to look at the signs over the door which indicated what work was done inside. A pair of scissors for a tailor, a gold lamb for a wool weaver, a basin for a barber, a painted wooden book for a bookbinder, a large swinging compass for an instrument-maker. Although more and more people were learning how to read, the artisans still had signs above their shops, not wishing to lose a possible patron merely because he happened to be illiterate.

When the British referred to early America as "a nation of farmers," they were only partially correct. While a majority of colonists

◆◆◆ This diagram of a silversmith's workbench was published in the 1771 *French Encyclopedia, or a Systematic Dictionary of Science, Arts, and the Trades* by Denis Diderot and Jean Le Rond d'Alembert. Artisans would catch scraps of silver in the workbench's leather aprons to reuse.

did tend gardens or crops, those who wanted to get ahead in the world also took up a trade. Many became artisans, called "mechanics" in the eighteenth century. They became bricklayers, carpenters, hatters, coopers, bakers, blacksmiths, and boat builders.

Forbes researched silversmithing extensively while writing *Paul Revere and the World He Lived In.* She describes Lapham's shop and the process of shaping silver with precise detail. Much of Paul Revere's work still exists in museums and private collections. Forbes probably also learned a great deal about printers and the publication of colonial newspapers. Good printers like Benjamin Edes were highly respected. They printed material such as handbooks, broadsides, and charts for private clients as well as for newspapers and magazines.

Dr. Warren was an enormously successful and popular doctor in Boston, largely as a result of his battle against a smallpox outbreak early in his medical career. Many colonial doctors, however, had little education in medicine. Medical knowledge was still limited, and doctors had not yet learned of the importance

Beautiful Writing

Many of the letters, reports, and other handwritten documents of the Revolutionary period have inconsistent spelling, grammar, and capitalization. This did not indicate that the writers were illiterate or poorly educated. Most people considered fine penmanship the most important aspect of writing. Spelling and grammar became more standardized when Noah Webster published his three-volume work *A Grammatical Institute of the English Language* from 1783 to 1785.

of good nutrition. Poor diet, bad sanitary practices, and harsh living conditions invited epidemics of diseases such as typhus and dysentery. Doctors had little success combating smallpox or scarlet fever, which today we can prevent by vaccination or cure by antibiotics. Common prescriptions for illness included bleeding, large doses of alcohol, raising blisters, and using plants such as rhubarb, hemp, vanilla, horseradish, and lavender.

Chapter 3

The Boston Tea Party

On November 29, 1773, the *Dartmouth* sailed into Boston Harbor carrying 114 chests of British tea. Two sister ships arrived soon after. The ships had been at sea for a month, out of touch with the news from the American colonies. Captain Hall did not expect any problems with the cargo. Although the Americans had vigorously resisted new British taxes, most of the tax acts had been repealed in the late 1760s.

Uproar in Boston

But Captain Hall found Boston in an uproar over the shipment of tea. Bostonians had begun debate over the tea more than a month before the ships arrived. The source of their complaints dated back to 1767, when Britain passed the Townshend Acts. These laws added duties, or taxes, to many imported goods. After the colonists rose up against the act, Britain repealed most of the duties. Only a small tea tax remained. Many Americans refused to buy taxed British tea.

In the summer of 1773, the powerful British trading giant, the East India Company, made plans to export shipments of surplus

◆◆◆ In *Paul Revere and the World He Lived In*, Esther Forbes describes Revere as "an engraver of propaganda pictures." In 1770, Revere published one of his best known prints, *Landing of the Troops* (detail shown here). Revere copied many of his images from other artists; this print was probably based on one by Christian Remick.

tea to America. The directors contacted Tories in America who would collect it in Boston and sell it to the colonists. These consignees would keep part of the profit. The *Dartmouth* and two other ships left for Boston in the fall.

On October 18, the patriotic *Boston Gazette* ran an article calling for the consignees to refuse the tea shipment. A week later, a number of newspapers printed an open letter attacking the tea tax as "the most dangerous stroke that has ever been meditated against the liberties of America." Opposition to the taxed tea imports grew steadily among the people of Boston. On November 1, the consignees received anonymous letters calling for them to resign publicly their commission to handle the tea.

One of the consignees was a merchant named Richard Clarke. Forbes may have used him as a model for her fictional character Jonathan Lyte. Both were wealthy Tory merchants who had country homes in Milton. They both fled to England in 1774.

The Patriot Mob

Clarke, along with the other consignees, disregarded the anonymous notes. On November 3, a crowd of patriots assembled in Clarke's warehouse to challenge the consignees. The mob took the hinges off the outer door and swarmed up the stairs. Clarke's allies managed to beat them back. After the conflict, the Sons of Liberty and other patriots issued even harsher attacks in newspapers. John Hancock led a committee that issued a set of resolves opposing the tea shipments. Governor Hutchinson held multiple meetings with the Governors Council. The members were unable to agree on a course of action.

The Tea Ships Arrive

The tension in Boston grew even higher when the *Dartmouth* sailed into Boston Harbor. The Sons of Liberty immediately printed up the "Friends! Brethren! Countrymen!" proclamation quoted in *Johnny Tremain*. The fictional Uncle Lorne did not print the copies, but he resembles Benjamin Edes, publisher of the *Boston Gazette*, in many ways. Edes's young son, Peter, mixed punch for gatherings of the Sons of Liberty. Unlike

Entitled *The Repeal, or the Funeral of Miss Ame Stamp*, this satirical cartoon shows British treasury secretary George Grenville and others responsible for the Stamp Act carrying it to a vault to be buried with other unjust acts. In response to the Stamp Act, colonists began a boycott of British goods, and Parliament soon repealed it.

Rab, a fictional character, Peter did not learn many of the organization's secrets.

Esther Forbes vividly describes Boston's mood at the time.

Almost every day and sometimes all day, the mass meetings at Old South Church went on. Tempers grew higher and higher. Boston was swept with a passion it had not known since the Boston Massacre three years before. Riding this wild storm were Sam Adams and his trusty henchmen, directing it, building up the anger until, although the matter was not publicly mentioned, they

would all see the only thing left for them to do was to destroy the tea.

The root of the crisis lay with the export and duty laws. The patriots would not allow the tea to be unloaded, and they clamored to have it sent back to England. But once in Boston Harbor, the tea was subject to the duties. The customs men would not let the ships leave with the tea on board unless the duties had been paid. If the ships stayed in the harbor for three weeks without paying duties, the customs men could confiscate the cargo. They would sell the taxed tea to the public.

Sam Adams and the patriots held mass meetings in the Old South Church. Governor Hutchinson tried to keep order in the seething city. Francis Rotch, owner of the *Dartmouth*, vainly

John Singleton Copley

John Singleton Copley, a Loyalist, volunteered to act as a mediator between the consignees and the angry Bostonians. He was Richard Clarke's son-in-law and one of the greatest portrait painters of his day. His diplomatic attempts ended in failure, but he is still remembered for his lifelike paintings of key historical figures, including that of Paul Revere seated at his workbench. Copley eventually moved to London.

requested a clearance from the customs men so that the ship could depart. Volunteer patriots, including Paul Revere, kept watch of the ships at night. The consignees fled in fear to Castle William, a fort outside of Boston. The tea did not budge from the harbor.

On December 16, 7,000 people attended a meeting at Old South Church. Dr. Warren and Josiah Quincy both gave speeches. Quincy cautioned the crowd to think of the consequences of any rash actions: "Let us weigh and consider before we advance to those measures which must bring on the most trying and terrific struggle this country ever saw." The meeting ended with Sam Adams's words: "This meeting can do nothing more to save the country." Rowdy groups dispersed with war whoops and cries of "To Griffin Wharf!"

Attending the Boston Tea Party

Today, we do not know all of the names or the exact number of people who took part in the Boston Tea Party. None of the participants wrote a detailed description immediately after the event. At the time, they would have been guilty of treason, punishable by hanging. Historians know the details from newspaper articles, letters, diaries, and accounts written many years after the event.

About 150 people, perhaps as many as 200, took part. Forbes gives the impression that the plot included a large number of

Americans throwing the Cargoes of the Tea Ships into the River, at Boston

When the British House of Commons passed the Tea Act on April 27, 1773, to help pay debts England had incurred during the French and Indian War, the American colonists became enraged. On December 16, 1773, a group of patriots boarded the East India Company's tea ships docked in Boston Harbor and dumped 342 chests into the water. Britain retaliated by issuing harsh legislation known as the Intolerable Acts.

apprentices and other boys, but most of the participants were in their twenties and thirties. A number of teenagers and other volunteers joined in as the group headed to the harbor. Many of them probably did not know of the plans beforehand. They would not have had time to put together elaborate costumes and probably only rubbed coal dust on their faces and hands. Many did not even wear costumes. Paul Revere and Benjamin Edes attended. Samuel Adams and John Adams most likely stayed away. Their part as organizers had ended.

The party began at 6 PM. Groups boarded each of the three ships. The men had smeared their faces with soot or grease. They wore ragged clothes and hoods over their heads. Johnny mentions sewing feathers on a hat to create a more "authentic" Indian costume, but there is no report that any participants actually used feathers.

The ship captains stood back as the men came aboard and hoisted the tea up from the hold. The raiders used their axes to chop open the chests, which were then tossed overboard. One man tried to tuck tea into his clothing, as Dove attempts in *Johnny Tremain*, but he was caught and punished. Another rowed a canoe around the ships and tried to shovel mounds of floating tea into his boat! A few of the raiders jumped over the side of the ship and tipped the man's canoe.

News of the activities at the harbor quickly spread around town. Thousands gathered at the dock to watch. British officials ordered their soldiers to stay away from the Boston Tea Party. Another clash like the Boston Massacre would have caused outcry and even rebellion across the colonies.

The Boston Tea Party ended at 9 PM. Ninety thousand pounds of tea bobbed in Boston Harbor. However, as the triumphant men headed home from the night's work, Admiral Montague warned them from a window that they would soon pay for their actions.

Chapter 4

The Road to War

A week after the Boston Tea Party, the *Gazette* reported a triumph: "A number of brave and resolute men, determined to do all in their power to save their country from the ruin which their enemies had plotted, in less than four hours emptied every chest of tea on board the three ships commanded by the captains Hall, Bruce, and Coffin, amounting to 342 chests, into the sea!! without the least damage done to the ships or any other property." Governor Hutchinson took a different view. He wrote to a friend, "There never was greater tyranny in Constantinople than has been lately in Boston."

The British Retaliate

On January 19, 1774, John Hancock's ship *Hayley* reached Britain, bearing accounts of the Boston Tea Party. Angry British government officials spent much of the spring drawing up measures to punish Bostonians. The Boston Port Bill was the first of four bills known together as the Coercive Acts or Intolerable Acts. The second bill amended the Massachusetts charter, giving Britain the right to appoint officials and banning

◆◆◆ **George III of England ruled from 1760 to 1820. He suffered from a disease called porphyria, which created bouts of madness and instability. Known for being stubborn, he was blamed for England's loss of the thirteen colonies. However, during his reign, England took control of India and Canada.**

town meetings. Another bill allowed the governor to halt trials and move them to Britain or another colony. A fourth permitted British soldiers to lodge in the homes of private families.

Bostonians learned of the Port Bill in May, shortly before General Thomas Gage arrived with four regiments of troops. The harbor was closed on June 1, the same day that Governor Hutchinson left for England. He would never return to America. Gage took office as governor. Over the summer, seven more regiments occupied Boston.

The Patriots Defy the British

The Coercive Acts heightened the determination of patriots across the colonies to defy the British. Johnny mentions that "from one end of the Atlantic seaboard to the other, towns and even villages sent great shipments of food," but cooperation

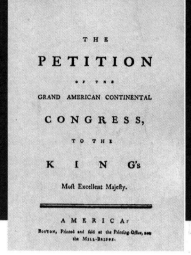

Members of the First Continental Congress *(left)* meet in Philadelphia in 1774. The congress included fifty members elected by twelve colonies. In 1775, the Second Continental Congress sent the Olive Branch Petition *(right)* to King George III, hoping he would help establish peace between Britain and the colonies. King George rejected it, calling it an illegal document written by an illegal congress.

between colonies went beyond food aid. Patriots in every town and city urged their countrymen to take action. After a summer of planning and negotiating, the Continental Congress met on September 6 in Philadelphia. Their most significant action was the adoption of the Suffolk Resolves, drafted a month earlier by Dr. Warren. The resolves formally condemned Britain's retaliation against Boston and recommended boycott of British goods. The resolves, going even further than passive resistance, called for patriotic citizens to "use their utmost diligence to acquaint themselves with the art of war as soon as possible, and do, for that purpose, appear under arms at least once every week."

The Call to Arms

This call to arms made a public summons for American troops to muster, but many towns had begun organizing militias in the spring of 1774. In *Johnny Tremain*, Rab spent Saturdays training with the Lexington militia. The sprawling Silsbee clan is fictional, but Forbes may have based the family on the Parkers of Lexington. More than a quarter of the Lexington minutemen were related in some way to the Parkers. Captain Robert Parker led the force, and one of the older members was Jonas Parker, probably a model for the determined Grandsire Silsbee.

Like Captain Parker, a veteran of the French and Indian War, many of the American colonists had some military experience. In the fall of 1774, a handful of colonies called up their militias that had fought during the 1760s. Many officers were Tories, however, and would not fight against the British. In Massachusetts, the patriots called for all officers to resign their posts. They were replaced by a popular vote, which ousted all Tories. Other colonies followed Massachusetts's example in creating militias loyal to the patriot cause.

Part of the military preparations included the creation of elite minutemen companies within the militias. The patriots did not expect much time to prepare when the British finally took action against the rebels. The minutemen would be ready at a minute's notice to march against an attack. Very young men and men not fit for combat were put on the "alarm list." They helped keep watch and performed any other duties needed to bolster the regular troops.

In December 1774, General Gage made it a crime of treason to stockpile arms. The Massachusetts forces disregarded the decree. They continued to stockpile arms and other supplies in the towns of Concord and Worcester. Still, they could not supply enough muskets for the members of their militias, which would handicap the rebels until well into the war. Like Rab, some tried to buy muskets from British soldiers. Many succeeded.

The British greatly underestimated the resolve and military ability of the patriot forces. In a letter describing the American soldier, a British officer wrote that "whenever it comes to blows, he that can run fastest will think himself best off."

The seizure of Fort William and Mary in Portsmouth, New Hampshire, shocked and infuriated the British. It came less than a month after Gage forbade stockpiling. In *Johnny Tremain*, Johnny's spying helps uncover British plans to assign more men to guard the British fort. A letter carelessly discarded by a British officer reveals a destination sixty miles away.

"Sixty miles," said Mr. Lorne. "That's Portsmouth. Fort William and Mary. They only have a handful of men on duty there and a vast store of powder and ball."

Gage's Spies

General Gage organized a network of informers and spies that gathered information almost as effectively as the patriots. They kept him informed on rebel plans, locations, and stockpiling of weapons. On one well-known excursion, Colonel Francis Smith, who appears briefly in *Johnny Tremain*, joined young Private John Howe. Posing as workers looking for jobs, they planned to ask around for work as they walked from Charlestown, just outside Boston, to Worcester. On the way, they stopped in Watertown for lunch. Colonel Smith's adventure ended when the serving girl addressed him by name! Howe later wrote of his exploits in *The Journal Kept by John Howe, as a British Spy*, published in 1827. Since the 1980s, some historians have believed that Howe's diary was really a fictional account based on the experiences of real people.

The Death of Warren, **shown above, appeared as the frontispiece in Hugh Henry Brackenridge's** *The Battle of Bunker-Hill.* **Printed in Philadelphia in 1776, the volume is subtitled** *A dramatic piece of five acts, in heroic measure. By a gentleman of Maryland.* **The picture is thought to be an accurate depiction of what the patriots wore during this famous battle.**

That night, over icy roads and through howling winds, Paul Revere rode the sixty miles. Even before the British got into their transports, word had come back to Boston that the King's Fort at Portsmouth had been seized and His Majesty's military stores stolen by rebellious Americans. The local militia had no trouble overwhelming the five men posted at the fort and seizing the supplies of arms and gunpowder. Afterward, the British in Boston kept a close eye on Paul Revere.

Gage had his own problems in Boston, too. His men had nicknamed him "Old Woman Gage." He did not impose censorship or curfews, nor did he arrest the patriot leaders. King George III of Britain, who wanted to see the colonies humiliated and brought to heel, called him "the timid general." Nonetheless, many colonists considered Gage a tyrant.

On the other hand, some of Gage's soldiers agreed with the patriot cause. The fictional Pumpkin tells Johnny why he wants to risk being shot for desertion: "Boy, I like it here. I want to live here forever. A farm of my own. Cows. Poor folk can't get things like that over in England." Americans earned higher wages than the British and with hard work could better their positions. Almost every day, at least one and sometimes a handful of soldiers sneaked out of the British camp during the night. At first, General Gage dealt leniently with those who were caught. His stance on deserters hardened after he pardoned Robert Vaughan. Shortly afterward, Vaughan deserted a second time, escaping successfully. Captured deserters were thereafter hanged or shot.

Antagonism between the British and the colonists worsened in Boston through the winter of 1774–1775 and the following spring. Paul Revere and his patrol continued monitoring the actions of the British, but most of the leaders left Boston during March. John Hancock and Sam Adams went to stay in nearby Lexington. Only Dr. Warren remained in Boston.

Chapter 5

Paul Revere's Midnight Ride

Before Paul Revere made his famous midnight ride, he was well known to patriots as an express rider. He carried news, messages, and warnings to towns far and wide. Express riders were faster and more dependable than the dawdling postal system. Revere made his first known express ride shortly before the Boston Tea Party. He was an excellent horseman and rode thousands of miles for the patriot cause. Johnny Tremain also serves as an express rider and once "rode as far as Worcester," forty-seven miles out of Boston and the town in which Forbes wrote *Johnny Tremain*.

On April 15, 1775, Paul Revere made a routine ride to Lexington. He had news of British activity to report to Hancock and Adams. The British had launched transport boats near the Boston-to-Charlestown ferry. General Gage had relieved his troops of regular duties to "learn Grenadier exercises and further new evolutions." Dr. Warren sent along a warning to hide the arms and supplies at Concord, since he believed the British would march soon.

At left is the **Old North Church**. Built in 1723, it is the oldest church building in Boston. It was here, on April 18, 1775, that Robert Newman, church sexton, hung two lanterns to tell colonists that British soldiers were approaching by sea. Pictured on the right is a lantern similar to those used on that historic night.

The Famous Signal

Before Revere returned to Boston, he stopped in Charlestown to meet with Colonel William Conant, a Son of Liberty. They devised a signal system in case the British departed Boston. The troops could leave by two routes. Boston was surrounded by water on three sides, connected to the mainland by a strip of land called the Neck. The British could march over the Neck, or they could row across the Charles River, dock at Charlestown, and march from there. Revere told Conant, "If the British went out by water we would show two lanterns in the North Church steeple—and if by land one as a signal." The North Church was the tallest building in Boston, easily visible from Charlestown. If riders could not get out of Boston, the patriots at Charlestown would know to spread the warning.

Gage planned to send his men out toward Concord on the evening of April 18 to seize the rebels' munitions, but he kept this secret even from some of his own officers. Patriot spies easily figured out his plan, however, including Johnny.

So . . . The campaign would start around eight that night. The Colonel's horse would be put on and off a boat. There would be a risk at least of drums and shooting. They were not going farther than thirty miles. Those men who thought the target of the expedition was going to be Lexington and Concord were right. And it would be Colonel Smith who would go in command.

A stable hand like Johnny did pass along the word of the British plan and destination. Paul Revere had already heard this information from two other sources!

"Two If by Water"

British troops started marching toward the Charles River at about 9:30 that night. Revere met quickly with Dr. Warren, who had

This map of the Boston and Concord areas was published in London in 1775. It includes an index, locating strategic points of interest, as well as the locations of recent military engagements between the British and Americans.

already sent Billy Dawes out to alert the countryside. Dawes was to sneak out via the Neck, while Revere would cross the Charles River and ride from Charlestown. Both would head to Lexington, warn Adams and Hancock, and continue on to Concord. Before he left, Revere called on Robert Newman, who lit two lanterns in the spire of North Church.

Thomas Richardson and Joshua Bentley rowed Revere across the Charles River. They moved very quietly, careful not to draw the attention of the British. Troops were still crossing the river, and the warship *Somerset* was moored in the middle

◆◆◆ **Although less well-known than Paul Revere, William (Billy) Dawes** *(left)* **also played an important role as an express rider on the night of April 18, 1775.**

of the river to watch for any rebels trying to leave Boston. Revere's small boat avoided detection. After landing, Revere met up with Colonel Conant and other Charlestown Whigs. They had a swift horse saddled for his ride. One man, Richard Devens, warned Revere that he had seen mounted British officers patrolling the roads.

"The Regulars Are Coming!"

Revere rode toward Lexington, turning abruptly at a fork in the road when he spied two British officers watching for express riders. He easily outran the heavier British horses and continued on to Lexington on a different road. In his own words, Revere "alarumed almost every house till I got to Lexington." There, he knocked on the door of the house where Hancock and Adams were staying. Eight militiamen guarded the house, and Sergeant

William Munroe asked him not to make so much noise. "You'll have noise enough before long! The Regulars are coming out!" Revere retorted. He gave Hancock and Adams the news, and Billy Dawes arrived shortly afterward.

Dawes and Revere continued toward Concord, soon joined by a Son of Liberty named Dr. Samuel Prescott, who was heading back to Concord from a visit with a young lady. The group was ambushed by a number of British soldiers who had been hidden in the trees. Dr. Prescott jabbed his horse with his spurs, jumped over a stone wall, and sprinted away before the British could react. Dawes attempted to do the same, but his horse threw him. He ran off into the woods on foot and escaped. The British blocked Revere's horse and captured him.

Meanwhile, Captain Parker mustered his minutemen in Lexington. They waited impatiently for further reports of the British approach. A few hours later, the British freed Revere outside of Lexington and took his horse. He returned to Lexington and again reported to Hancock and Adams. The two leaders decided to leave before the British arrived. They departed Lexington in a carriage, along with Revere and Hancock's secretary, John Lowell. In their haste, Hancock left behind a trunk full of important papers. Revere and Lowell returned to retrieve the trunk. They had to pass through the crowd of minutemen assembled around a meetinghouse and headed out of town lugging the trunk as the first shots sounded at Lexington.

Chapter 6

The Beginning of the American Revolution

The British reached Lexington early on the morning of April 19. A force of more than 700 redcoats faced about 77 minutemen. Colonel Francis Smith and Major John Pitcairn led the British troops. Gage had chosen the portly Smith to command, according to Forbes, because "he had been in service longer than any of the other (and smarter) colonels." Both Tories and Whigs liked Pitcairn, the "tough old marine" famous for his profanity. Many Bostonians mourned after he was killed in the Battle of Bunker Hill.

The Patriots Face the British

The minutemen spread out in a line on Lexington Common. More than half of the assembled men belonged to Captain Parker's Lexington militia. Onlookers stood nearby or peeped out of house windows.

Major Pitcairn ordered the rebels to disperse. Captain Parker supposedly proclaimed, "Don't fire unless fired on, but if they mean to have a war let it begin here." In an official account, however, he stated that he only "ordered our Militia to disperse and not to fire." Major Pitcairn commanded his men to surround and disarm the small group of rebels.

Chaos broke out when someone fired a shot. Historians still debate about which side fired that first shot. The British responded with a volley of fire, and many soldiers broke rank and charged toward the rebels. Pitcairn unsuccessfully tried to rein back the British soldiers. The force responded only when Colonel Smith appeared from the rear of the ranks and had a drummer beat out a signal. By the time the troops came to order, every bystander had vanished. The officers ordered the British onward to Concord.

Eight minutemen had been killed, though no British soldiers were even seriously wounded. Among the dead lay old Jonas Parker. Residents quickly emerged from nearby houses to tend the wounded, nine in all. Captain Robert Parker prepared to lead his remaining force to defend Concord.

The March to Concord

Patriots in Concord had begun preparing for the arrival of the British after Dr. Prescott arrived with the warning. The minutemen assembled, messengers rode out to alert other towns, and citizens worked to hide any remaining military supplies. They had heard of the shooting in Lexington but probably did not yet know that eight men had been killed. Two hundred fifty members of the militia marched to meet the British. A short distance away from the advancing troops, they wheeled and marched back to Concord! The British entered Concord escorted by the minutemen, musicians of both groups playing fifes and beating drums.

Battle of Lexington

The mission began peacefully. Colonel Smith and Major Pitcairn took most of their troops into Concord to search for stores of weapons and other patriot supplies. After the Lexington incident, officers had warned the men to refrain from any violence in their search. As a result, they missed as many supplies as they found. The remainder of the British soldiers marched toward North Bridge under the command of Captain Parsons. He further divided the forces, taking half to search for munitions at a nearby farm and leaving only 100 to guard the North Bridge.

The Shooting Begins

Concord had hillier terrain than Lexington. Militia members were able to assemble out of sight of the British. More and more men arrived throughout the morning, and a large force gathered on a ridge overlooking North Bridge. At about 10 AM, the rebels noticed smoke wafting from Concord. Smith's men were burning some of the supplies they had found, but the militiamen believed that the British had set fire to the town. About 400 men stormed down the hill toward the small British force at the bridge.

The British had no time to get into battle formation. Captain Walter Laurie sent a message to Colonel Smith for reinforcements.

After the fighting at Lexington, Ralph Earl and Amos Doolittle visited the battleground. Doolittle gathered eyewitness accounts as Earl painted the landscape. Combining Earl's paintings with accounts of the battle, Doolittle created four engravings. Pictured here is plate IV, *The South Part of Lexington.*

The minutemen began to cross the bridge toward the British, and a few panicked British soldiers fired. The rebel force responded, driving the British back in a retreat toward Concord. They met the rotund Colonel Smith coming with reinforcements. The combined force managed to drive off the minutemen, and they regrouped in Concord. Three British soldiers lay dead, and a number of rebels had been killed or wounded. Nearly an hour later, Captain Parsons and his men returned safely from searching the farm. They had stopped by a tavern on the way back!

The British waited in Concord for more troops to arrive. After his men interrogated Paul Revere the previous night, Colonel

◆◆◆ **Battle Road, as it looked in 1917, follows the route of the bloodiest fighting of April 19, 1775. As the British returned to Boston from the skirmishes in Concord and Lexington, they were ambushed by farmers who shot at them from behind stone walls, trees, barns, and houses.**

Smith had sent a messenger to Gage asking for a backup force. They had not appeared by noon. Rebels across the countryside, from more than forty towns, were converging on Concord. Colonel Smith gave the order to march.

Battle Road

Rebels waylaid the British as they took the road toward Lexington. Instead of acting in formation, they shot from the side of the road. The tired and bewildered British did not know which direction to aim. They ran low on ammunition. Many started to run, even as their exhausted and wounded comrades desperately tried to keep moving.

Lord Percy's force finally met Colonel Smith in Lexington. Lord Percy took command, and the troops stopped to regroup. The fresh force's heavy weapons kept the rebels at bay. At 3:45 or so, the British were ready to continue their march.

One of Percy's men, Lieutenant Frederick MacKenzie, wrote a thorough account of the day's events. "Our men had very few opportunities of getting good shots at the rebels," he said of the retreat, "as they hardly ever fired but under cover of a Stone wall, from behind a tree, or out of a house; and the moment they had fired they lay down out of sight until they had loaded again, or the column had passed. In the road indeed in our rear, they were most numerous, and came on pretty hard, frequently calling out, 'King Hancock Forever.'" Their attackers included Captain Parker's Lexington militia. The British retaliated by shooting back and burning some houses along the road, now known as Battle Road. Lord Percy's troops finally reached Charlestown at 8 PM. At the end of the day, seventy-three British soldiers and forty-nine Americans had been killed.

British Atrocities

Dr. Warren heard of the shooting even before General Gage. He left Boston to join the militia and arrived at Lexington at about the same time as Percy's troops. After Adams and Hancock departed, he became the patriot leader of Boston. The day after the battle, he began spreading the word about the "barbarous murders." He quickly circulated a notice throughout the colony that asked citizens to "give all assistance possible in forming an army." Rumors of horrible British atrocities spread throughout the colonies. Thousands of men converged on Boston, and Dr. Warren drew up formal terms of enlistment into the Massachusetts service. A couple of days later, he took depositions from the militiamen, witnesses, and British captives. From these, an official report was drawn up and sent around the colonies and to Britain. Newspapers blazed headlines such as "Bloody Butchery by the British Troops."

Patriot Heroes

The battle made martyrs of the patriots, even though the British had sustained greater casualties. In the eyes of most colonists, the British had destroyed property and started the bloodshed. At

Chain of Errors

On the night of April 18, a sleepless General Gage worried about the troops leaving for Concord. At 3:00 in the morning, he sent an order to General Lord Hugh Percy to march out with his brigade to support Colonel Smith. Through poor communication, a servant left the message on a table instead of delivering it personally. When Smith's rider arrived, Gage awoke General Percy and sent for the four regimental commanders of his brigade.

One of these commanders was Major Pitcairn of the marines. Gage had forgotten that he had appointed Pitcairn as Colonel Smith's second in command! By the time the British figured out their mistake and called up the marines, Lord Percy's departure had been delayed four crucial hours.

the same time, the rebels had proved that they could triumph over the British, who had been considered nearly invincible. The colonists began to unite in support of the patriots. In *Johnny Tremain*, after the incident Johnny swallows his shame over his wounded hand and lets Dr. Warren examine it. The doctor is guardedly optimistic.

> "I don't know whether you can ever go back to your silver work. But not even Paul Revere is going to make much silver for a while."
> "Will it be good enough to hold this gun?"
> "I think I can promise you that."
> "The silver can wait."

Likewise, many colonists left their work to join the revolution. Sam Adams and John Hancock headed to the Second Continental Congress in Philadelphia. There, delegates elected George Washington commander in chief of the newly established army. Many still balked at taking action against Britain. In slightly more than a year, however, some of the same people would meet again in Philadelphia to declare independence from Britain.

Glossary

act A formal order issued by lawmakers.

artisan A skilled worker or craftsman.

atrocity A brutal or cruel act.

broadside A single sheet of paper printed on one side that often told sensational news of the day and sold for a cheap price.

Committee of Correspondence Group organized in a colonial city or town to spread opposition to and plan protests of British rule.

common An open plot of land set aside for public use, similar to a park.

consignee One to whom something is shipped to be sold; agent.

deposition Official testimony taken down in writing.

duty A tax, often on imported goods.

martyr One who dies for a cause he or she believes in.

militia A body made up of armed citizens, not of professional soldiers.

munitions Materials used in war, such as weapons and ammunition.

regular A full-time soldier.

resolve Determination, or a formal resolution.

treason An act of betrayal or of trying to overthrow one's country.

tyranny Oppressive power exercised by the government.

For More Information

Massachusetts Historical Society

1154 Boyleston Street

Boston, MA 02215-3695

(617) 535-1608

Web site: http://www.masshist.org

The Paul Revere House

19 North Square

Boston, MA 02113

(617) 523-2338

Web site: http://www.paulreverehouse.org

Web Sites

Due to the changing nature of Internet links, the Rosen Publishing Group, Inc., has developed an online list of Web sites related to the subject of this book. This site is updated regularly. Please use this link to access the list:

http://www.rosenlinks.com/lal/joht

For Further Reading

Fink, Sam. *The Declaration of Independence*. New York: Scholastic Reference, 2002.

Forbes, Esther. *America's Paul Revere*. Boston: Houghton Mifflin Company, 1946.

Fradin, Dennis Brindell. *Samuel Adams: The Father of American Independence*. New York: Clarion Books, 1998.

Hakim, Joy. *From Colonies to Country* (History of US, Book 3). New York: Oxford University Press Children's Books, 1999.

Lawson, Robert. *Ben and Me: A New and Astonishing Life of Benjamin Franklin As Written by His Good Mouse Amos*. Boston: Little, Brown & Co., 1939.

Bibliography

Birnbaum, Louis. *Red Dawn at Lexington.* Boston: Houghton Mifflin Company, 1986.

Forbes, Esther. *Johnny Tremain.* Boston: Houghton Mifflin Company, 1943.

Forbes, Esther. *Paul Revere and the World He Lived In.* Boston: Houghton Mifflin Company, 1942.

Griswold, Wesley S. *The Night the Revolution Began: The Boston Tea Party, 1773.* Brattleboro, VT: Stephen Greene Press, 1972.

Larabee, Benjamin Woods. *The Boston Tea Party.* New York: Oxford University Press, 1964.

Randel, William Peirce. *The American Revolution: Mirror of a People.* Maplewood, NJ: Hammond Inc., 1973.

Rhodehamel, John, ed. *The American Revolution: Writings from the War of Independence.* New York: The Library of America, 2001.

Tourtellot, Arthur Bernon. *Lexington and Concord: The Beginning of the War of the American Revolution.* New York: W. W. Norton & Company, 1959.

Unger, Harlow Giles. *John Hancock: Merchant King and American Patriot.* New York: John Wiley & Sons, 2000.

Wilbur, C. Keith. *Revolutionary Medicine 1700–1800.* Philadelphia: Chelsea House Publishers, 1980.

Wolf, Stephanie Grauman. *As Various as Their Land: The Everyday Lives of Eighteenth Century Americans.* Fayetteville, AR: University of Arkansas Press, 2000.

Primary Source Image List

Page 5 and cover (top): 1937 photograph of Esther Forbes. Housed at the American Antiquarian Society in Worcester, Massachusetts.

Page 6: Frontispiece in the first edition of *Johnny Tremain*, 1944. It was painted by Lynd Ward.

Page 8: *The Bloody Massacre perpetrated in King Street Boston on March 5, 1770 by a party of the 29th Regt.* Paul Revere.

Page 10 (left): Notice advertising Paul Revere's work as a dentist. It appeared in the *Boston Gazette* on September 19, 1768. Housed at the Massachusetts Historical Society.

Page 10 (right): John Singleton Copley, American, 1738–1815, *Paul Revere*, 1768. Oil on canvas, 89.22 x 72.39 cm (35 1/8 x 28 1/2 in.), Museum of Fine Arts, Boston, gift of Joseph W. Revere, William B. Revere and Edward H. R. Revere, 30.781.

Page 11: The Paine tea service, 1773, commissioned by Dr. William Paine of Worcester for Lois Orne. Executed by Paul Revere. Housed at the Worcester Museum of Art in Worcester, Massachusetts.

Page 12 (left): Portrait of Joseph Warren by Edward Savage. Copied in oil on panel from the 1765 original by John Singleton Copley. It is owned by the Museum of Fine Arts, Boston.

Page 12 (right): John Singleton Copley, American, 1738–1815, *Samuel Adams*, about 1772. Oil on canvas, 125.73 x 100.33 cm (49 1/2 x 39 1/2 in.), Museum of Fine Arts, Boston, deposited by the City of Boston, L-R 30.76c.

Page 15: 1773 engraving of the Green Dragon tavern, Boston, Massachusetts.

Page 19: Front page of the *Boston Gazette* from January 1, 1770, Boston, Massachusetts.

Page 20: Title page of *An Oration Delievered March 15, 1774, At the Request of the Inhabitants of the Town of Boston: To Commemorate the Bloody Tragedy of the Fifth of March 1770. By the Honorable John Hancock, esq.* Printed in 1774 by Edes and Gill in Queen Street, Boston, Massachusetts. Housed at the Massachusetts Historical Society.

Page 21: Portrait of Thomas Hutchinson, engraving, circa 1765.

Page 22: Plate 27 from *The Frugal Housewife, or Complete Woman Cook.* Written by Susannah Carter, it was published originally in London. First published in the colonies by F. Newbery, it was reprinted by Edes and Gill of Boston.

Page 25: *A Westerly View of the Colleges in Cambridge New England*, also identified as *Plate 9, Colleges in Cambridge, 1767.* Engraved by Paul Revere.

Page 26: An engraving of a silvershop workbench from the *French Encyclopedia, or a Systematic Dictionary of Science, Arts, and the Trades* by Denis Diderot and Jean Le Rond d'Alembert. Published in 1771.

Page 29: *A View of Part of the Town of Boston in New England and British Ships of War Landing Their Troops 1768,* engraved, printed, and sold by Paul Revere.

Page 31: *The Repeal, or the Funeral of Miss Ame Stamp,* engraved by Benjamin Wilson, 1766. Housed at the Library of Congress Prints and Photographs Division, Washington, D.C.

Page 34: *Americans throwing the Cargoes of the Tea Ships into the River, at Boston,* engraved by W. D. Cooper, 1789. Housed at the Library of Congress, Division of Rare Books and Special Collections, Washington, D.C.

Page 37: *George III, King of England* (1760–1820), anonymous. Housed in Chateaux de Versailles et deTrianon, Versailles, France.

Page 38 (left): Engraving depicting the First Continental Congress in Carpenters Hall, Philadelphia, Pennsylvania. Engraved in 1774 by Francois Godefroy, printed in the *Journal of the Proceedings of the Congress, held at Philadelphia, September 5, 1774,* published 1774.

Page 38 (right): Title page for *The Petition of the Grand American Continental Congress, to the King's Most Excellent Majesty.* Printed by Isaiah Thomas of Boston, 1774.

Page 41: *General Thomas Gage,* 1788, housed at the Yale Center for British Art.

Page 42: *The Death of Warren,* etching, frontispiece of Hugh Henry Brackenridge's *The Battle of Bunkers-Hill.* Printed and sold in Philadelphia in 1776. Housed at the Library of Congress, Washington, D.C.

Page 47: Hand-colored map, published in London, 1775, inscribed "to Richd. Whitworth by J. De Costa; C. Hall, sc." Housed at the Library of Congress, Geography and Map Division, Washington, D.C.

Index

About the Author

Corona Brezina, a graduate of Oberlin College, is a musician and writer living in Chicago.

Photo Credits

Cover (top), pp. 5, 22, 25, 29 courtesy, American Antiquarian Society; cover (bottom left), pp. 34, 42 Library of Congress Rare Book and Special Collections Division; cover (bottom right), p. 6 from *Johnny Tremain* by Esther Forbes, with illustrations by Lynd Ward, copyright © 1943 by Esther Forbes Hoskins, renewed 1971 by Linwood M. Erskine, Jr., Executor of the Estate of Esther Forbes Hoskins, reprinted by permission of Houghton Mifflin Company, all rights reserved; p. 8 Library of Congress Prints and Photographs Division; pp. 10 (left), 12 (left), 13, 20 courtesy of the Massachusetts Historical Society; pp. 10 (right), 12 (right) photographs ©2003 Museum of Fine Arts, Boston; p. 11 Worcester Art Museum, Worcester, Massachusetts, Gift of Frances Thomas and Besie Sturgis Paine in memory of Frederick William Paine; pp. 15, 38 (right) © Bettmann/Corbis; pp. 19, 21, 38 (left) © Hulton/Archive/Getty Images; p. 26 Boston Public Library/Rare Books Department, courtesy of The Trustees; p. 31 © Corbis; p. 37 Giraudon/Art Resource, NY; p. 45 (left) courtesy of the Bostonian Society/Old State House; p. 45 (right) image supplied by the Commission of the Old North Church; p. 47 Library of Congress Geography and Map Division; p. 48 © Burstein Collection/Corbis; p. 53 Print Collection, Miriam and Ira D. Wallach Division of Art, Prints and Photographs, The New York Public Library, Astor, Lenox and Tilden Foundations; p. 54 courtesy of the Concord Free Library.

Designer: Les Kanturek; Editor: Jill Jarnow; Photo Researcher: Cindy Reiman